QUINLAN V. KANE

Third Edition

Quinlan V. Kane

Third Edition

Frank D. Rothschild

Attorney at Law
Kilauea, Hawaii

Deanne Siemer

Attorney at Law
Wilsie Co. LLC
Washington, D.C.

Anthony J. Bocchino

Professor of Law
Temple University
Beasley School of Law
Philadelphia, Pennsylvania

NITA®

THE NATIONAL INSTITUTE FOR TRIAL ADVOCACY

Address inquiries to:
Reproduction Permission
National Institute for Trial Advocacy
1685 38th Street, Suite 200
Boulder, CO 80301
(800) 225-6482 Fax (720) 890-7069
permissions@nita.org

ISBN 978-1-60156-216-6
FBA 1216

14 13 12 11   10 9 8 7 6 5 4 3 2 1

Printed in the United States of America

CONTENTS

FACT SUMMARY

Roberta Quinlan is a business broker who specializes in the buying and selling of electronics manufacturing and sales firms. Business brokers are agents for buyers or sellers of businesses, and generally work on a commission basis. Quinlan has been a broker in the electronics industry for fifteen years. Kane Electronics was a chain of retail electronics outlets located throughout the State of Nita in twenty-six locations. Its president, founder, and sole shareholder was Brian Kane. On August 4, 2011, Kane Electronics was sold to Nita Computer World, a national retailer of computers and other electronic business equipment, for $10 million of Nita Computer World stock. Roberta Quinlan claims that she served as the broker for this transaction and that she had an agreement with Brian Kane to do so. She claims that the agreement was reached during a business meeting held at Kane's house on June 12, 2011, and was set out in a confirming letter that she mailed to Kane that day; she also maintains that she contacted Cliff Fuller of Nita Computer World on behalf of Kane Electronics and was responsible for putting Nita Computer World and Kane together, which is what business brokers do. She has sued Kane for $300,000, 3 percent of the closing value of Kane Electronics, per her agreement with Kane.

Kane and Quinlan have known each other for about ten years, mainly as golf partners. Kane admits that he decided to sell his business in early June and that he told Quinlan of his decision during a round of golf on June 11. Kane admits he invited Quinlan to his house the next day to talk about the sale of his business. Kane admits he had several conversations with Quinlan about the possible sale of his company over the years, but he says they were all preliminary and brainstorming in nature. Kane denies there was an agreement between him and Quinlan for her to act as his agent. He admits to receiving a letter from Quinlan shortly after their meeting in which Quinlan attempted to confirm an agreement he says they never reached. He says he wrote the word "unacceptable" in all capital letters on this letter, signed it, and had it immediately mailed back to Quinlan. She denies ever receiving this mailing, and assumed as a result that he was agreeable to her working on his behalf to sell his business. Kane admits that when he was first contacted by phone by Cliff Fuller of Nita Computer World on June 27, 2011, Fuller said he had been referred by Roberta Quinlan. He also admits that he did not know Fuller, or of Nita Computer World's interest in his company, before the Fuller phone call. Kane maintains he negotiated his own deal with Nita Computer World, that he entered into no contract with Quinlan for her to act as his broker in the sale of his business, and therefore does not owe Quinlan a commission.

IN THE DISTRICT COURT OF THE FIFTH CIRCUIT
STATE OF NITA

ROBERTA QUINLAN,	)	
	)	
Plaintiff,	)	
	)	
v.	)	CIVIL ACTION NO. 1298
	)	
BRIAN KANE,	)	
	)	
Defendant.	)	
	)	

COMPLAINT FOR DAMAGES

JURISDICTION

1. This Court has jurisdiction over this action pursuant to 5 Nita Stat. Ann. §552(a)(4)(B).

VENUE

2. Venue is proper pursuant to 5 Nita Stat. Ann. §553(b).

PARTIES

3. Plaintiff, Roberta Quinlan, is a citizen of the State of Nita and is more than 18 years of age, and at all times relevant was engaged in an enterprise as a business broker specializing in the buying and selling of electronics manufacturing and retail firms.

4. Defendant Brian Kane is a citizen of the State of Nita and is more than 18 years of age. Until August 4, 2011, when he sold the business, Defendant was the president, founder, and sole shareholder of Kane Electronics.

STATEMENT OF FACTS

5. In June 2011, Defendant, as its sole shareholder, decided to sell Kane Electronics.

6. On June 12, 2011, Defendant met with Plaintiff in her professional capacity as a business broker to discuss the sale of Defendant's business.

7. During that meeting Defendant agreed to engage Plaintiff as the broker for the sale of Kane Electronics.

8. Defendant agreed that dependent on the amount of effort required by the Plaintiff that he would pay her a minimum fee of 3 percent of the closing value of the sale of Kane Electronics.

9. On June 13, 2011, Plaintiff mailed a letter to Defendant, at his business address, postage pre-paid, confirming the agreement referred to in paragraph 7 above pursuant to which Plaintiff would broker in the sale of Defendant's business.

10. Thereafter, in her capacity as a professional business broker, Plaintiff identified Nita Computer World as a potential buyer for the Defendant's business.

11. Plaintiff telephoned Cliff Fuller, General Counsel of Nita Computer World, to inform him of the availability of Kane Electronics for purchase and inquire about the interest of Nita Computer World in making such an acquisition.

12. On June 27, 2011, at the suggestion of Plaintiff, Cliff Fuller called Defendant to speak about the potential purchase of Defendant's business by Nita Computer World.

13. But for the call from Plaintiff, Cliff Fuller did not know of Defendant's interest in selling his business and Defendant did not know that Nita Computer World was a potential buyer of his business.

14. Upon information and belief, Cliff Fuller, on behalf of Nita Computer World, and Brian Kane, on behalf of Kane Electronics, negotiated the terms of the sale of Kane Electronics to Nita Computer World.

15. On information and belief, on August 4, 2011, Nita Computer World bought Kane Electronics.

16. On information and belief, Nita Computer World paid Defendant ten million dollars ($10,000,000) for Kane Electronics.

17. Thereafter, Plaintiff demanded the Defendant pay her commission of 3 percent of the sale proceeds of $10,000,000, or $300,000.

18. Defendant has refused to make the agreed upon payment referred to in Paragraph 17 above.

COUNT I

BREACH OF CONTRACT

19. Plaintiff hereby incorporates Paragraphs 1-18 by reference as though the same were set forth at length.

20. By failing to pay Plaintiff the agreed upon commission for her broker services in the sale of Kane Electronics, Defendant has breached his contract with the Plaintiff.

WHEREFORE, Plaintiff requests that this Court:

(1)   Award Plaintiff $300,000 in damages, plus pre-judgment interest.

(2)   Award Plaintiff her costs and reasonable attorney's fees in this action as provided by 5 Nita Stat. Ann. § 552(a)(4)(E); and

(3)   Grant such other and further relief as this Court may deem just and proper.

Respectfully submitted,

Leland A. Bell

Leland A. Bell
Nita City Tower, Suite 801
5 Main Street
Nita City, NI 99992
555-726-6269
Nita Bar No. 12088

Dated: October 21, 2011

IN THE DISTRICT COURT OF THE FIFTH CIRCUIT
STATE OF NITA

ROBERTA QUINLAN,   )
)
Plaintiff,   )
)
v.   )   CIVIL ACTION NO. 1298
)
BRIAN KANE,   )
)
Defendant.   )
_____   )

ANSWER

For his answer to the Complaint in this action, with respect to each numbered paragraph therein,

Defendant Brian Kane states as follows:

1.   Admitted.

2.   Admitted.

3.   Admits that Plaintiff Roberta Quinlan is a citizen of the State of Nita and is more than eighteen years of age. States that Defendant has insufficient information on which to admit or deny that Plaintiff is an experienced business broker who specializes in the buying and selling of electronics manufacturing and sales firms.

4.   Admitted.

5.   Admitted.

6.   Admits that on June 12, 2011, Defendant met with Plaintiff and denies all other allegations of Paragraph 6.

7.   Denied.

8.   Denied.

9.   Admits that Plaintiff mailed a letter to Defendant dated June 13, 2011. Denied that there was any agreement between Plaintiff and Defendant regarding broker services in the sale of Kane Electronics. By way of further response Defendant states that upon receipt of the aforementioned letter that Defendant wrote the word "UNACCEPTABLE" on the bottom of the letter and mailed the letter back to the Plaintiff, postage prepaid to Plaintiff's business address in an envelope with a printed return address of the business address of the Defendant.

10. States that Defendant has insufficient information on which to admit or deny the allegations that Plaintiff identified Nita Computer World as a potential buyer for the Defendant's business.

11. States that Defendant has insufficient information on which to admit or deny the allegations that Plaintiff telephoned Cliff Fuller to inform him of the availability of Kane Electronics for purchase.

12. Admits that on June 27, 2011, Cliff Fuller called Defendant about the sale of Defendant's business and denies all other allegations of Paragraph 12.

13. Admits that on June 27, 2011, Defendant did not know that Nita Computer World was a potential buyer of his business, and denies all other allegations of Paragraph 13.

14. Admitted.

15. Admitted.

16. Admitted.

17. Admits that Defendant refused to pay Plaintiff's commission, which amounted to 3 percent of the sale proceeds of $10,000,000, or $300,000.

18. Denies that Plaintiff was or is entitled to any commission.

19. Admitted.

20. Denied.

Respectfully submitted,

Leslie Randall

Leslie Randall
425 Main Street
Nita City, NI 99992
555-726-1931
Nita Bar No. 3098

Dated: November 18, 2011

DEPOSITION SUMMARIES

DEPOSITION SUMMARY OF ROBERTA QUINLAN

1   My name is Roberta Quinlan. I am forty-eight years old and a lifelong resident of Nita City. I have
2   been married to William Feldman for twenty-five years. He is a partner with the law firm of Parker
3   & Gould in Nita City. We have two children who are grown and on their own. I have both a BS and
4   an MBA in business from Nita University. I began my career as a business broker once the kids were
5   in middle school. My job is to put buyers and sellers of businesses together and help them reach
6   sales agreements. Over the past fifteen years I have developed an expertise in companies and busi-
7   nesses involved in the electronics industry, both manufacturers and retailers of these products.
8
9   I have known Brian Kane for about ten years. We met in 2002 when he asked me to play in a
10   mixed foursome golf tournament with him at the Rolling Green Golf Club where we both are
11   members. We are both avid players, and since that time, we have regularly entered tourna-
12   ments together as well as playing together socially. I have played since college where I was
13   on the golf team. Even though Brian took up the game later in life, he is a natural athlete and
14   fierce competitor, so we make a very good team and have been quite successful. These photos
15   you have shown me, marked Exhibit 7 and Exhibit 8, are of Brian and me playing in the club
16   championship round in the early summer last year before all this happened.
17
18   About five years ago Brian, who is now in his early fifties, started talking to me about possibly
19   selling his business, Kane Electronics. Of course I already knew all about his business, includ-
20   ing that he started it on a shoestring in 1983 after working for Wellfleet Digital Manufacturing,
21   Inc. for a few years, and that he had expanded to twenty-six retail outlets throughout the state
22   of Nita. He also knew about my business and my expertise in the electronics industry. These
23   conversations usually occurred after our round of golf. We had an understanding that we never
24   discussed business on the golf course. He seemed really torn between his love for his work and
25   a strong feeling of guilt at not spending more time with his family.
26
27   On June 11, 2011, Brian told me during a round of golf that he had finally decided to sell
28   his business. I knew by then that he and his wife were having troubles, and he told me he
29   desperately wanted to be able to spend more time with his family and get his marriage back
30   together. I told him I would be pleased to discuss the sale and give him some advice on how
31   to proceed. As I said, Brian knew all about my business, but there was no talk of retaining me
32   at that point. Instead, he asked that I come by his house the next day, which was a Sunday,
33   so that we could talk more about the sale of his business.
34
35   I got to his house about noon. We immediately went to the study, which I knew was his home office,
36   and met for about two hours. We first talked about the value of the company. He had already
37   obtained appraisals and based on those said that he hoped to get somewhere in the neighborhood
38   of $8 to $10 million for his business. Based on the appraisals of his company and my knowledge of
39   the industry, I told him that $8 million was low and that $10 million was a realistic goal for the
40   sale. We then talked about the possible forms such a sale could take. I explained that because

1 he was the sole owner of the company, the sale could be accomplished by selling all of the
2 stock to the buyer for cash, by selling all of the assets of his company to the buyer for cash,
3 by exchanging his stock for shares of stock in a corporate buyer, or by some combination of
4 these methods. As it turned out, his preference was to exchange his stock for stock of the
5 buying company if he could find a growing company as a buyer.

Page 35

1. Q: As I understand it, you talked with Mr. Kane at his house in June of last

2. year, not at his office?

3. A: Yes, he wanted to meet right away on Sunday, so he suggested his home,

4. which was more convenient for both of us.

5. Q: The two of you discussed various options on how he might sell his business?

6. A: Among other things, yes.

7. Q: What else did you talk about?

8. A: As I said, we went over the appraisals and my advice on the appropriate

9. selling price. We also talked about what I would charge as a brokerage fee.

10. Q: Who brought up the topic of fees?

11. A: I did. I told Brian that the range of fees for a deal such as what he was

12. interested in was 3 to 5 percent, depending upon the level of involvement

13. by the broker.

14. Q: What did he say to that?

15. A: Nothing really, I think we just moved on to another topic.

16. Q: What was that topic?

17. A: We talked about the kind of buyer we would be looking for—stable,

18. on the rise, that sort of thing. I told him I had a lot of contacts in the industry and

19. I was sure I could find an appropriate buyer.

20. Q: What was his reaction?

21. A: He said, "I'm aware of your reputation Roberta." I assured him that I would

22. do some checking around on his behalf that next week. At that point, Brian's

23. wife came in and reminded him of a social engagement and we cut our

24. meeting short. As I was leaving, I told him I'd call him next week or so. I believed

25. that Nita Computer World was a potential buyer and intended

26. to check that out.

Page 36

1. Q: When at his house, you did not tell Mr. Kane that you had someone in mind

2. who might be interested, did you?

3. A: No. I didn't want to raise premature expectations.

4. Q: Did Mr. Kane ask you to check with your contacts in the industry?

5. A: No, but he didn't say not to.

6. Q: And he didn't say that you should do some checking either, did he?

7. A: Not in so many words, no.

8. Q: Did you believe that Mr. Kane had contracted for your services at that point?

9. A: Not formally, that's why I wrote him that same day.

10. Q: But he never said "You're hired" or "I want to hire you to help sell my business"

11. or anything like that, did he?

12. A: Brian never said we had a deal explicitly, but he also didn't tell me not to go

13. forward on his behalf, either.

40 As I was leaving, I told Brian that given the excellent shape his company was in, I felt as
41 though we could proceed fairly quickly to a desirable conclusion. I knew that Nita Computer
42 World was actively acquiring smaller retail outlets and thought that they were a potential
43 buyer for Brian's company. I was familiar with Nita Computer World because my husband had
44 handled a number of acquisitions for them in late 2010 and early 2011.

1   While I would have preferred it, the fact is we didn't sign a contract that day, but it was clear to me we
2   had a deal. When I got home that evening I wrote and mailed a letter to Brian setting out our agree-
3   ment. The letter, marked as Exhibit 3, is dated June 12, 2011. I kept a copy for my files. The other let-
4   ter in my files to Kane, also dated June 12, 2011, and marked as Exhibit 2, is a copy of my first draft of
5   my letter to Kane. After I read it over, I realized it wasn't accurate as to our agreement so I wrote and
6   sent Exhibit 3. I don't even know why I kept Exhibit 2—I should have discarded it with the original. I
7   also talked with my husband that night about Nita Computer World as a possible purchaser, and he
8   suggested I call Cliff Fuller, general counsel at Nita Computer World, whom I had met recently at a
9   social event at my husband's firm. Exhibits 9 and 10 are photos of Cliff and me at that event.
10

11   The document you have shown me with the heading "Broker Agreement" at the top, Exhibit 5,
12   is a form contract that I usually use in signing up clients. My husband's law firm prepared
13   this for me so that the terms of the agreement with the client would be clear. In Brian's case,
14   given our relationship as friends, I decided to use a letter instead of the form contract. I don't
15   remember any other recent deal in which I used a letter, but my relationship with Brian out-
16   side of business was unique among recent clients. I regard a letter as being just as good and
17   as binding as if we had filled out one of my agreement forms shown in Exhibit 5.
18

19   When I didn't hear back from Brian wanting to change our agreement as spelled out in my
20   letter, I moved forward as his broker. I never received any communication from Brian and I
21   certainly did not receive my letter back from him with the word "unacceptable" written on
22   it. If I had I wouldn't have contacted Cliff Fuller that next week and arranged for him to call
23   Brian. Exhibit 4 is my phone log for June 24, 2011. It shows that call, and the call I made to
24   Brian telling him to expect a call from Cliff Fuller. I keep a log on my computer that I fill in
25   as I'm making phone calls at the office, and this is a printout of that log for that date. While
26   I didn't actually talk with Brian that day, I did leave a message on his voice mail saying to
27   expect a call from Fuller. I tried to call him again later that day, as shown by my phone log, but
28   this time I spoke with his secretary who said, after checking, that Brian wasn't in. I decided
29   not to leave another message other than that I had called.
30

31   I found out through my husband that Cliff Fuller did call Brian and that there was mutual
32   interest right off the bat. I called Brian several times after that, but he didn't return any of
33   my calls. No, I don't have phone logs for those calls. I must have called from someplace other
34   than the office, probably on my cell phone. I am told they started working on a deal immedi-
35   ately and that the negotiations went smoothly. I was not involved at all in these negotiations,
36   but I was responsible for putting Fuller and Kane together. That's what a broker does. It's for
37   that reason that I deserve the minimum fee that I set out in my contract letter to Brian. Usu-
38   ally the broker will be more involved in the negotiations, but I have had other deals like this
39   where the principals do their own negotiations. It's for that reason that once Kane and Fuller
40   were talking I didn't insert myself into the proceedings. I was always available if needed. I did
41   not have to do a lot of work, obviously, but in my business it's often the work you've done
42   over the years and who you know, not how much work you do on the particular assignment,
43   that makes or breaks a deal. Brian Kane got top dollar for his business, consistent with my
44   advice to him, and if I had not called Cliff Fuller the deal would never have happened.

1 After waiting three weeks from when I heard the deal closed, and hearing nothing from Brian, I
2 emailed him asking for my commission. Exhibit 12 is my saved copy of that email. His response,
3 which is Exhibit 13, shocked me. He never mailed me a marked-up copy of my letter agree-
4 ment. He's making that all up to get out of paying me what I'm owed. It's unfortunate this has
5 happened, and that I've had to sue a former friend to get the fee I deserve.

I have read this deposition and it is complete and accurate.

Roberta Quinlan

Roberta Quinlan
1/17/2012

DEPOSITION SUMMARY OF BRIAN KANE

1   My name is Brian Kane. I am fifty-four years old and have lived here in Nita City all my life.
2   My wife Elvira and I are currently separated, and our three beautiful teenage daughters live with
3   her most of the time. I get them every Wednesday evening and two weekends a month. I bought
4   a condo near our family home so there would be as little interruption in the girls' lives as possible.
5   After I graduated from Nita University in 1980 with a business degree, I worked three years for
6   Wellfleet Digital Manufacturing, Inc., at their Boulder, Colorado, facility before deciding to set out
7   on my own in the retail electronics business. I moved back to Nita City, and with the help of some
8   friends and family and a bank, I scraped together enough money to open my first retail electron-
9   ics store in 1983. Back then I sold television and stereo equipment. When the computer industry
10   started to grow, I rode that wave, which in part fueled the opening of addtional stores. Through a
11   lot of hard work and good timing, the business expanded over the years to where I ended up with
12   twenty-six locations all over the state. I was the president, founder, and sole shareholder of the
13   company during all the years before I sold it.
14
15   For the first fifteen years of being in business, my life was my business. I had little time for outside
16   activities, even dating. Then in 1995 I met Elvira, a customer who wanted to register a complaint
17   with the "boss" of the company. We married not long afterwards. Bianca, our first child, was born
18   in 1996. Rachel was born in 1998, and Terry in 2000. Not long after Rachel's birth, I decided I
19   needed something to take my mind off of the grind of work, so I took up golf, and it became a real
20   passion. I am very competitive and played whenever I could, usually twice a week in the summer
21   and I would often hit golf balls at the club driving range after work or over lunch.
22
23   It was through golf that I met Roberta Quinlan. After I joined Rolling Green Golf Club in about
24   2001, I remember seeing her on the driving range hitting balls and was very impressed. She
25   could really hit a golf ball. I first met her on the driving range when she offered me a tip on my
26   grip and I later learned she played on the Nita University golf team. Not long after, I asked her
27   if she would be my partner in a mixed foursome tournament and that started a long friendship
28   centered around golf. She was a lot of fun to play with and had the same kind of competitive
29   spirit that I have, which resulted in a number of trophies for us both. Exhibits 7 and 8 are pho-
30   tos of Roberta and me at the club.
31
32   I was also impressed with Roberta's knowledge of business. We often talked about both our
33   businesses, and I would pick her brain with ideas I had for expansion and the occasional thought
34   of selling my business so I could do something else. Over the years, talk of my selling out was
35   more frequent as I became more disenchanted with being unable to spend quality time with
36   my family and Elvira's discontent with that fact. Like the many other real estate and business
37   brokers that I have dealt with over the years, Roberta tended to be a little too aggressive in
38   her own self-promotion. My experience with brokers over the years has been that they are, at
39   best, a necessary evil, but I never have liked the way they hit you up and try to push you into
40   giving them business.

1   In early 2011 I started having serious problems in my marriage. I began to reevaluate my
2   life and decided I had been spending far too much time at the office, and not enough
3   with my family. My daughters only had another few years before they would be out of
4   the house and in college, and if there was to be any chance of salvaging my marriage, I
5   needed to make some changes. By May I had committed in my own mind to sell out.
6   I hired a couple of appraisers to determine a fair price for my company. The appraisals come
7   in at a low of $8 million and a high of $10 million. I had also done some research on my own
8   and with the retail industry becoming more and more competitive I was happy with either
9   of those numbers. Armed with those appraisals, made a few calls to people I knew in the
10   industry, and put out feelers. Although I hadn't been successful as of then, my business was
11   in good shape, in an expanding market, and I was sure I could find a buyer in time.
12
13   The next time I saw Roberta, at a golf game in early June, I told her of my decision. She got
14   all excited and wanted to talk about nothing else the rest of the day. She urged me to let her
15   broker the deal, wanted to spend a few hours meeting with me after our round of golf, and
16   on and on. Just to get her to calm down and let me enjoy the golf game, I told her we could
17   talk about it the next day at my house. Even though I had no intention of hiring her because
18   I had decided to do this deal myself, I still felt as though I might learn something talking with
19   her given her experience as broker in the electronics industry, and I didn't want to hurt her
20   feelings by abruptly cutting her off and telling her she had no chance of getting this business.
21   I now regret that decision.
22
23   When she came over the next day, June 12, a Sunday, we went straight to my study, which
24   is where I work when I am at home. Exhibit 11 is a diagram of the layout of my house and it
25   shows the study where we met. Roberta was more than her usual aggressive self in trying
26   to get me to sign on the dotted line, so to speak, and make her my agent for this deal. I kept
27   putting her off, saying I had to think it all over. I must admit that I was trying to learn as much
28   as I could from her about how she thought the deal might be structured and how she saw
29   things working out best for me. But I had picked her brain for years on business deals without
30   ever hiring her. I definitely did not hire her at this meeting. We just talked. There were many
31   options discussed. At one point I do remember that she told me that her fee for helping me
32   would only be 3 to 5 percent and I tried to make her feel as though I thought that was very
33   reasonable. Of course, what I was really thinking was that by handling the sale myself, with
34   the help of my lawyers of course, I would be saving anywhere from $250,000 to $500,000
35   by bypassing a broker such as Roberta.

Page 22

1.   Q: Why didn't you just flat out tell Ms. Quinlan that you didn't want her as your

2.   agent on this sale?

3.   A: I didn't want to seem rude or harsh with my long-time friend and golf partner.

4.   Q: But didn't she tell you she'd be looking around for a buyer for your business?

5.   A: Yes, but I never told her she should. I thought that was just all part of her sales

6.   pitch.

7.   Q: Did you tell her not to?

8.   A: No, I didn't.

9.   Q: Did you encourage her to keep a lookout?

10. A: No, I didn't actively encourage her.

11. Q: What did you do then?

12. A: I learned long ago in business to keep my options open. I thought, who knows

13. what she might come up with, so I said nothing.

14. Q: What did you think she'd do based on this meeting?

15. A: Well, had I thought about it, I guess I should have known Roberta, as

16. aggressive as she is in business, would try to find someone to buy my business

17. and get the sizeable commission for the deal, but I never hired her

18. to do that for me. She took that upon herself without my approval.

1   Fortunately, my wife came into the study and reminded me of a social engagement. I was very
2   glad to end that meeting with Roberta. First she was very pushy, then she tried to guilt trip me
3   into hiring her, talking on and on about her contacts in the industry. That's what they all say,
4   you know. It felt like someone trying to get you to change phone companies, and I wanted no
5   part of it.
6
7   I got Roberta's so-called confirming letter later that week. Yes, Exhibit 3 is a copy of that letter. I
8   couldn't believe this attempt to cut herself in on my deal. There was no understanding between
9   us that needed confirmation. I had not hired her to do anything, so I wrote the word "unac-
10 ceptable" in all caps at the bottom of the letter, signed it, and gave it to my secretary, Peg, to
11 mail back to her. I'm sure Peg could tell that I was steaming mad. I also told Peg that if Roberta
12 called, she was to say I wasn't in. I really didn't like dealing with this side of Roberta's personality.
13 I was having enough trouble with one woman in my life and didn't need Roberta hassling me
14 too. Exhibit 1 is a telephone slip with my secretary's handwriting on it. I don't remember get-
15 ting this, but it is consistent with my instructions.

1   In late June I got a call from Cliff Fuller, the general counsel at Nita Computer World. I didn't
2   know him at all, nor did I have any idea that they might be interested in my company. Exhibit
3   6 is a note I made about Fuller's call. I did know the company, however, as a major player in
4   the electronics field, and recognized that they were large enough to be able to pay top dollar
5   for my business. Cliff told me in that first call that he had been told by Roberta to call me. It
6   never occurred to me that Roberta would expect to be compensated for this phone call given
7   that I had sent her letter back marked unacceptable. Mr. Fuller and I arranged to meet for
8   lunch. I don't recall whether Fuller suggested that Roberta join us. He might have, but there
9   was no reason for her to be there. Once Cliff and I talked, I learned that Nita Computer World
10   was planning to expand their retail operations to include more outlets that sold both Nita
11   Computer World products and products manufactured by other companies. This was news
12   to me, but good news, as I had established retail outlets that could easily add Nita Computer
13   World products to the line we already sold. I handled all of the negotiations myself just as I had
14   planned and after some back and forth and meetings with the lawyers, we arrived at a mutu-
15   ally agreeable arrangement whereby Nita Computer World bought my company in exchange
16   for $10 million of their stock. We probably had ten meetings in all, all without Roberta. It's true
17   that Roberta discussed that form of sale with me, but in the end, it was my tax lawyers who
18   persuaded me to close the deal in that form. The deal closed on August 4. I was ecstatic. Finally
19   I would have time to be with my kids, and try to make things right with Elvira, and then this
20   lawsuit got filed.
21
22   I received an e-mail from Roberta a few weeks after the deal with Nita Computer World
23   closed. That's Exhibit 12. It made me think of that old Ronald Reagan line, "There you go
24   again." I waited overnight to respond in order to cool down. Exhibit 13 is my email back to
25   her, in which I refused to pay her anything at all, given that she really did nothing to earn a
26   fee.
27
28   It's not the money that she's asking for that troubles me so much; it's the principle of the
29   thing. If I had wanted Roberta to be my agent, then I would have hired her and signed an
30   agreement specifically setting out our arrangement. That's how I have always done business,
31   in writing. I quickly learned some thirty years ago that's the only safe way to proceed. I never
32   agreed to hire her; instead she's trying to foist herself on me and my company and I don't like
33   it. And this has ruined a perfectly good golf team, too.

I have read this deposition and it is complete and accurate.

Brian Kane
1/18/2012

DEPOSITION SUMMARY OF CLIFF FULLER

1 My name is Clifford Fuller. I am forty-four years old, my wife's name is Maggie, and I have one
2 child, who is in high school. I am a lifelong resident of Nita, and I graduated from Nita Law
3 School. I live in the same house that I grew up in, and my father, who is quite old now, lives with
4 us. My first job out of law school was with the firm of Parker & Gould, where for many years I
5 worked with William Feldman, the husband of the plaintiff in this case. I didn't know his wife
6 Roberta very well because she only came to a few office functions during the years I was at the
7 firm. Exhibits 9 and 10 are photos taken at one of those functions. I never knew much about
8 her other than she worked as a business broker after their kids got older, and she went by her
9 maiden name of Quinlan.
10
11 About five years ago, I left the firm to take the position of general counsel with one of the firm's
12 biggest clients, Nita Computer World. I had represented Nita Computer World in quite a few
13 of their acquisitions during my years at the firm. It is now a very substantial company in the
14 electronics field. In my job as general counsel, I negotiate deals for the company, make sure we
15 are complying with state and federal regulations, and advise the officers and managers. I also
16 manage our outside counsel in litigation matters.
17
18 In late June of 2011, Roberta Quinlan called me at the office. After exchanging pleasantries, she
19 told me that an old friend and client, Brian Kane of Kane Electronics, was interested in selling his
20 business. She told me a few basic facts about the business, probably the gross revenues, number
21 of locations, and things like that. I don't remember specifically what she said, but she certainly
22 sounded knowledgeable. I know she mentioned that Kane had appraisals for his company in the
23 $10 to $12 million range, which initially seemed reasonable. She said she had heard that Nita
24 Computer World was acquiring businesses of this kind, and she asked me if our company might
25 be interested in such a purchase. I told her we definitely might be, but of course, we have a lot
26 of hoops to jump through when we are considering an acquisition. She talked about a deal for
27 stock, and said that Kane was interested in being acquired by a growing company. There is no
28 doubt that she spoke as if she was the broker for Kane Electronics, and I assumed she was.
29
30 She told me to call Brian Kane directly if we decided we were interested and gave me his office
31 and home phone numbers. This was a little odd because usually brokers like to make the intro-
32 duction. After talking with the necessary people at our company, I called Mr. Kane on June 27 and
33 we set up a lunch to talk things over. I know that I told him that I was calling at the suggestion of
34 Roberta Quinlan. I also asked if Roberta would be joining us for lunch and he said he'd see if she
35 was available. No, I didn't call Roberta about the meeting, that was Kane's call to make. Kane and
36 I hit it off right away. We talked about a deal for stock, and it was clear to me that we were both
37 on the same track. I later introduced him to our president and soon after we all met with their
38 lawyers. After some back and forth, there were probably ten meetings in all, we arrived at a price
39 and Nita Computer World purchased Kane Electronics for $10 million of our stock. The deal closed
40 in early August. We have been very happy with this purchase and I thought we got a great deal.

1   Yes, I guess I was a little surprised that I never heard from or saw Roberta Quinlan after that
2   initial phone call. I thought for sure, as the broker, she would at least sit in on some of the
3   meetings that led up to our agreement with Mr. Kane. I have no firsthand knowledge of what
4   their arrangement was; all I can go on is what Ms. Quinlan told me over the phone. I must say,
5   Mr. Kane never mentioned her at all in all of our dealings. Yes, I do remember telling Mr. Kane,
6   when we first spoke, that his broker had called me, and I identified her by name. He said he
7   often played golf with her, and we went on to talk about the deal. He didn't seem surprised
8   that I mentioned her. He didn't say anything to suggest she was his broker, but he didn't say
9   anything to suggest she wasn't his broker either.
10
11   Kane handled the deal basically by himself, only using lawyers to close the deal. He seemed
12   to have made up his mind what he wanted to do, and to me at least it did not appear that he
13   was relying on anyone's advice. This is unusual in my experience. Normally there are brokers
14   working on the deal, especially in the negotiation on price. He did have lawyers working on
15   the papers, but they seemed to be acting as functionaries and not as advisors, basically doing
16   what Kane told them. He's kind of a quiet person. He doesn't talk much, but seemed very
17   self-assured, and the people working for him pain close attention. He was a good person to
18   negotiate with. Once he said he'd do something, he didn't change his mind or try to renegoti-
19   ate the terms.

I have read this deposition and it is complete and accurate.

Clifford Fuller (signature)

Clifford Fuller
1/19/2012

Deposition Summary of Margaret Edmondson

1 My name is Margaret Edmondson, but I am usually called Peg. I am forty-four years old, mar-
2 ried with two children, and live at 1445 Old City Way in Nita City. Until August of 2011, I was
3 the secretary/administrative assistant to Brian Kane of Kane Electronics. I now work as an
4 office manager for Nita Computer World, the company that bought Mr. Kane's business. He
5 was instrumental in getting me my current job. In addition, when Mr. Kane sold his business,
6 I received a bonus of $50,000, which he said was for my years of hard work on his behalf.
7 Mr. Kane gave bonuses to about twenty of us who had been with him for many years.
8 I don't know what others received. I also took from the company a retirement plan that I had
9 paid into together with contributions from Kane Electronics. Although I no longer work for
10 Mr. Kane, it is fair to say that I remain loyal to him. He has always been a good and fair employer
11 for me and everyone else who worked for him.
12
13 I started work with Mr. Kane in 1987. At that point Kane Electronics was just one store in Nita
14 City, although the year I started we opened up two other stores in other parts of the city.
15 I was fresh out of high school where I had taken a business curriculum and I was hired to assist Mr.
16 Kane's secretary, Nancy Owens. When Nancy moved with her family out of state in 1992, I became
17 Mr. Kane's secretary. Over time, as my responsibilities grew with the business, I got the title of Admin-
18 istrative Assistant, although I always continued to do Mr. Kane's secretarial work. In that capacity my
19 job duties included Mr. Kane's word processing, his filing, his correspondence, and answering his
20 phones and taking messages when Mr. Kane was unavailable.
21
22 Kane Electronics grew to a chain of twenty-five stores throughout the State of Nita during
23 the time I worked there. I was always located at our main office that was originally in down-
24 town Nita City. Later, in 2003, we moved to an office complex Mr. Kane built called Kane Plaza.
25 Mr. Kane was in the office at least three days a week, although he was constantly on the road visiting
26 our other stores. Honestly, I don't know how he kept up the pace for as long as he did.
27
28 Mr. Kane was very successful in his business but it took a toll on his personal life. His wife and
29 three daughters are extremely important to him and I know he felt guilty about not spending
30 more time with them. His wife would frequently call for him at the office and would be irritated
31 if he wasn't there or if I wasn't able to put her through because he wasn't taking calls. I also
32 know that she resented his playing golf, which was his only recreation, because of the time it
33 took, especially when he played in tournaments with Roberta Quinlan. Mr. Kane started to talk
34 about selling out his business about six or seven years ago, more frequently as time went on.
35
36 In the spring of 2011, Mr. Kane definitely decided to sell his business. He had a conversation with me
37 about it, and was apologetic about it, but said that he had to try to save his marriage for the sake of his
38 children. I told him that he was right to sell, that his children had to come first. I think I was the first per-
39 son in the company to know about his decision because I was the one who arranged for appraisals and
40 the like, so Mr. Kane wanted me to know what was going on. I remember when the appraisals came

1   in. He had hired two different appraisers to be sure. As it turned out, both appraisals put a range of

2   valuation for the company at a little over $8 million as a low and a little over $10 million at the high

3   end. Mr. Kane was very pleased with the appraisals. He commented to me about the appraisals that

4   he hoped they were accurate; that he would sell in a minute for $8 million. I asked him what the

5   process would be and he told me that he intended to handle the sale himself, which was typical of

6   Mr. Kane. He often said that, "If you want something done right then you should do it yourself."

7

8   I was unhappy to hear about this lawsuit by Roberta Quinlan. In a way it was my fault. The

9   weekend after Mr. Kane got the appraisals, I knew he had a golf tournament with Ms. Quinlan

10   as his partner. I knew she was some sort of business broker and I suggested that Mr. Kane get

11   some tips from her; after all, they had been friends for years.

12

13   Shortly after the golf tournament, Mr. Kane received a letter from Ms. Quinlan. Yes, that's it,

14   Exhibit 3. I opened the letter, as I did all of his correspondence. I remember this letter specifi-

15   cally, first because it concerned the sale of the business, which was of utmost concern to us all

16   at the time, and second because of his reaction to seeing the letter. He called me into his office

17   and asked me to mail the letter back to Ms. Quinlan. He had written on the letter and signed

18   it. It was a one word note which said "unacceptable." I could tell he was very upset by this let-

19   ter by the way he ordered me to send it back. He also told me that if Ms. Quinlan called, that I

20   should tell her he wasn't in. I mailed Ms. Quinlan's letter marked by Mr. Kane on the same day

21   he gave it to me, using one of our envelopes, stamped, and to the same address Ms. Quinlan

22   had on her letterhead. It was never returned, so I assume she got it. No, I didn't make a copy

23   of that return letter. I wish I had.

24

25   Sure enough Ms. Quinlan called not long afterwards, and per Mr. Kane's instruction, I took a

26   message, even though Mr. Kane was in his office. Exhibit 1 is that message. Shortly thereafter,

27   Mr. Kane got a call from a Mr. Fuller at Nita Computer World. Mr. Kane was real excited about

28   the lunch meeting they scheduled and told me that he might have lucked out and the sale might

29   happen quicker than even he had hoped. He also thanked me for suggesting that he talk to Ms.

30   Quinlan because apparently Mr. Fuller heard about Mr. Kane's company being available from her,

31   or at least so he said. After the meeting he was even more optimistic.

32

33   Mr. Kane and Mr. Fuller met together several times themselves and over time others were

34   involved including the lawyers to finalize the deal. Roberta Quinlan never participated in any

35   of those meetings to my knowledge, and because I was the one to check everyone's schedule

36   for meetings, I'm sure I would have known if she had. I know that Mr. Kane intended to do

37   this deal, like all the others he did, by himself.

I have read this deposition and it is complete and accurate.

Margaret Edmondson

Margaret Edmondson
1/20/2012

JURY INSTRUCTIONS
AND
VERDICT FORM

Jury Instructions

1. The Court will now instruct you about the law that governs this case. By your oath, you agreed to accept and follow these instructions and to apply them to the facts you find from the evidence. Any verdict in this case must be the unanimous decision of all jurors.

2. The plaintiff, Roberta Quinlan, claims that the defendant, Brian Kane, breached a contract to pay her for services as a business broker. The defendant, Brian Kane, denies that claim.

3. As the plaintiff, Roberta Quinlan has the burden of proving her claim by a preponderance of the evidence, which is the greater weight of the evidence or the evidence that you find is more believable.

4. To prevail on her claim, the plaintiff, Roberta Quinlan, must show (a) she and Brian Kane made an agreement or contract that she would perform services as a business broker, and he would pay her an agreed amount or the reasonable value of those services, (b) she performed the agreed services, and (c) he failed to pay her the amount due.

5. An agreement or contract can be formed by one or more writings, oral statements, or conduct which collectively demonstrates that each of the parties agreed to the same terms.

6. When one party offers credible evidence that a letter was correctly addressed and properly mailed in the United States mail, that party is entitled to a rebuttable presumption that the letter was received by the party to whom it was addressed. In this case, the party to whom the letter was addressed has denied receiving it. You, as the trier of fact, must weigh the presumption of receipt against the denial of receipt and decide whether the letter was received.

7. If you find that the plaintiff, Roberta Quinlan, proved her claim by a preponderance of the evidence then your verdict should be for the plaintiff, and you should determine the amount she is due as damages according to the terms of that agreement or contract.

8. If you find that the plaintiff, Roberta Quinlan, failed to prove her claim by a preponderance of the evidence, then your verdict should be for the defendant, Brian Kane.

IN THE DISTRICT COURT OF THE FIFTH CIRCUIT
STATE OF NITA

ROBERTA QUINLAN,   )
)

Plaintiff,   )
)

v.   )   CIVIL ACTION NO. 1298
)

BRIAN KANE,   )   VERDICT FORM
)

Defendant.   )
_____   )

We, the jury, unanimously find:

MARK AN "X" ON THE CORRECT LINE.

IF YOUR VERDICT IS FOR THE PLAINTIFF, FILL IN AN AMOUNT THERE.

_____ For the plaintiff, Roberta Quinlan, in the amount of $ _____.

_____ For the defendant, Brian Kane.

_____

                                               Foreperson

EXHIBITS

Exhibit 1

IMPORTANT MESSAGE

For _Brian_

Day _6/24_   Time _2:30_   A.M.
                                    P.M.

M _A. Quinlan_

Of _____

Phone _225 · 6482_
FAX   Area Code   Number   Extension
MOBILE _____
       Area Code   Number   Extension

Telephoned	✓	Returned your call		RUSH	
Came to see you		Please call		Special attention	
Wants to see you		Will call again		Caller on hold	

Message _Told her you were not in — as per your instructions_

Signed _Peg_

Universal 48023   LITHO IN U.S.A.

Exhibit 2

ROBERTA QUINLAN
Business Broker
12 Meredith Lane
Nita City, NI 99992
(555) 225-1922
roberta@robertaquinlan.nita

June 12, 2011

Mr. Brian Kane
One Kane Plaza
P.O. Box 626
Nita City, NI 99992

Dear Brian:

It was a pleasure to visit with you this afternoon concerning the sale of Kane Electronics. As I told you, I am confident that I can find an appropriate purchaser of either the assets or the stock of the company, although I understand that you are also open to an exchange of your stock in Kane for stock in a company with a good investment future.

During our conversation, we agreed that I would use my best efforts and contacts (which are many) to find a suitable purchaser of Kane Electronics. Upon consummation of any sale, regardless of its nature or form, which results from my efforts, Kane Electronics will pay me an amount to be decided upon at a later date, but in no event less than 3 percent of the net closing value to the seller.

I will be in touch with you from time to time.

Warm regards,

Roberta Quinlan

rq/s

Exhibit 3

ROBERTA QUINLAN
Business Broker
12 Meredith Lane
Nita City, NI 99992
(555) 225-1922
roberta@robertaquinlan.nita

June 12, 2011

Mr. Brian Kane
One Kane Plaza
P.O. Box 626
Nita City, NI 99992

Dear Brian:

It was a pleasure to visit with you this afternoon, and I write to confirm our understanding.

You, as the sole shareholder of Kane Electronics, desire to dispose of your stock holdings in the company by way of an exchange of shares of a corporation with a good investment future. If I arrange for such an exchange, which is acceptable to you, Kane Electronics will pay me a fee calculated at between 3-5 percent of the closing value, dependent upon my time and effort necessary on your behalf.

If I do not hear from you, I will assume that this arrangement is acceptable to you. I already have a prospect in mind and will be in touch with you in the near future.

Warm regards,

Roberta

Roberta Quinlan

rq/s

Exhibit 4

ROBERTA QUINLAN
Business Broker

Outgoing Phone Log

Date	Person Called	Telephone #	Business Purpose
6/24	Cliff Fuller	287-1440	Called re: potential interest in Kane Electronics. Says NCW looking to acquire companies like Kane. Thinks Kane may already be on their list of potential acquisitions. He will call Kane.
6/24	Brian Kane	877-2893	Called to tell him expect call from Cliff Fuller at NCW. Left message on voice mail.
6/24	Brian Kane	877-2893	Called again, Secretary claims isn't in. I hope he isn't ducking me to try to get out of our agreement (don't be paranoid)

Exhibit 5

ROBERTA QUINLAN
Business Broker

BROKER AGREEMENT

AGREEMENT made this ___ day of _____, by and between Roberta Quinlan, Business Broker, 12 Meredith Lane, Nita City, NI 99992, hereinafter "broker," and _____, hereinafter "customer."

In consideration of the mutual agreements hereinafter contained and other good and valuable consideration, the sufficiency and adequacy of which are hereby acknowledged, the parties hereto agree as follows:

1. The term of this contract is six months (180 days) from the date that appears above.

2. Customer hereby retains the Broker to locate a buyer or seller as appropriate for the requirements of the Customer.

3. Broker hereby undertakes to use best efforts to locate a buyer or seller as appropriate for the requirements of the Customer. Broker makes no guarantee or warranty of success with respect to any such efforts.

4. If the Broker locates a willing buyer or a willing seller as appropriate for the requirements of the Customer, the Broker has completed performance under this Agreement and is entitled to the fee described in paragraph 5.

5. Customer hereby agrees to pay to Broker a fee of ____% of the total selling price for the business, including the fair market value of any stock, stock options, warrants or other consideration of any kind, at the closing of the sale, in cash, by certified check, or by wire transfer.

6. This agreement shall inure to the benefit of, and shall be binding upon, the parties hereto and their successors and assigns. This Agreement shall be governed by the laws of the State of Nita. This Agreement may be executed in one or more counterparts, which, taken together, shall constitute the whole agreement, and there may be duplicate originals of this Agreement.

IN WITNESS WHEREOF, this Broker Agreement has been duly executed by the parties hereto as of the date first above written.

WITNESS:

_____   _____

                                        Roberta Quinlan, Broker

_____   _____

                                        Customer

Exhibit 6

**From the desk of
Brian Kane**

6/27

ph fr Cliff Fuller
Gen'l Counsel NCW

Roberta referred

Sounds promising - Knows about
appraisals, Roberta ??

Lunch Thursday @ Pucks

ph = 287-1440

Exhibit 7

Exhibit 8

Exhibit 9

Exhibit 10

Exhibit 11

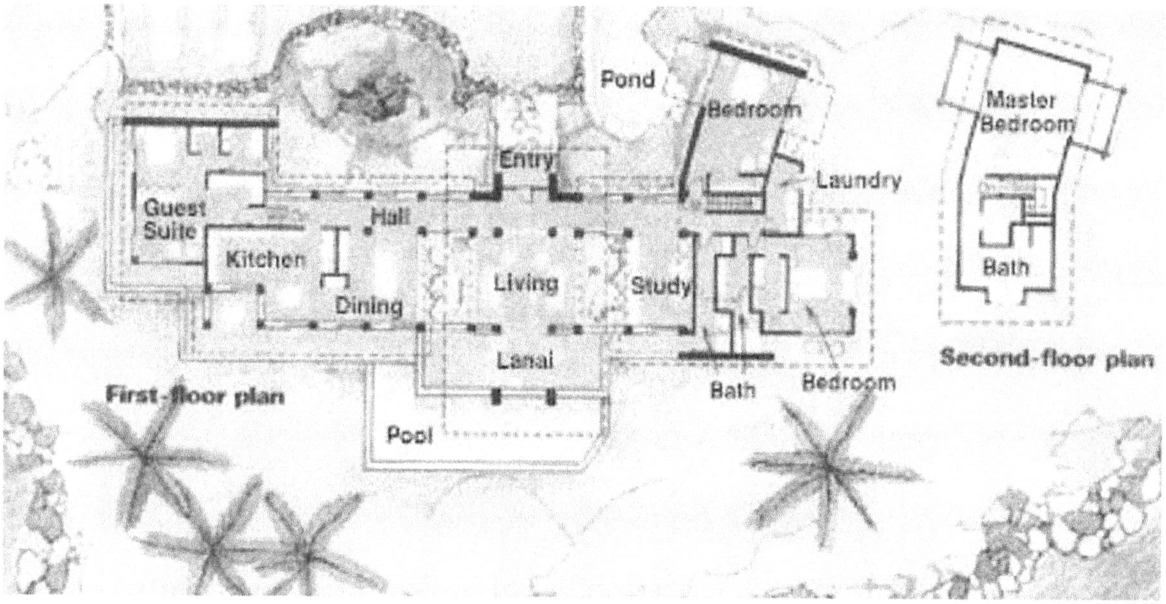
Pond
Bedroom
Entry
Laundry
Guest Suite
Hall
Kitchen
Living
Study
Dining
Lanai
First-floor plan
Bath
Bedroom
Pool
Master Bedroom
Bath
Second-floor plan

Exhibit 12

Roberta Quinlan

From: Roberta Quinlan roberta@robertaquinlan.nita

Sent: Thursday, August 25, 2011 9:23 AM

To: Brian Kane (bk@kaneelectronics.nita)

Subject: **Commission re sale to NCW**

Brian: I can't believe I haven't heard from you since you closed the deal with NCW. Such great news, and at such a great price! I thought this would be a good match, and I certainly was right. Now you can concentrate on mending fences with Elvira and the girls, just as you wished. Because my actual time in putting this deal together was relatively small, under our letter agreement dated June 12, 2011, I am only asking for the minimum commission of 3% of the closing value, which is $300,000, if what I hear is correct, that the ultimate sale price was $10,000,000.00. When can I expect a check?

Roberta

Roberta Quinlan
Business Broker
12 Meredith Lane
Nita City, Nita 99992
(555) 225-1922
roberta@robertaquinlan.nita

Exhibit 13

Brian Kane

From: Brian Kane bk999@gmail.nita

Sent: Friday, August 26, 2011 10:45 AM

To: Roberta Quinlan

Subject: what commission?!

Roberta: I can't believe you think you are owed a commission on the NCW deal. We had no agreement, letter or otherwise. Yes, I did receive your June 12 letter and I immediately had my secretary mail it back to you after I personally marked it "UNACCEPTABLE" and signed it.

I thought that would put to rest your attempts to take part in and benefit from the sale of my business, which I intended all along to do myself. That's why I avoided your later efforts to inject yourself into the process. I do thank you for sending Mr. Fuller my way, which I considered an act of a friend. How wrong I was!

Brian

Brian Kane
1046 Nottingham Way
Nita City, Nita 99993
bk999@gmail.nita

From: Roberta Quinlan roberta@robertaquinlan.nita

To: Brian Kane bk@kaneelectronics.nita

Sent: Thursday, August 25, 2011 9:23 AM

Subject: Commission re sale to NCW

Brian: I can't believe I haven't heard from you since you closed the deal with NCW. Such great news, and at such a great price! I thought this would be a good match, and I certainly was right. Now you can concentrate on mending fences with Elvira and the girls, just as you wished. Because my actual time in putting this deal together was relatively small, under our letter agreement dated June 12, 2011, I am only asking for the minimum commission of 3% of the closing value, which is $300,000 if what I hear is correct, that the ultimate sale price was $10,000,000.00. When can I expect a check?

Roberta

Roberta Quinlan
Business Broker
12 Meredith Lane
Nita City, Nita 99992
(555) 225-1922
roberta@robertaquinlan.nita

SPECIAL IMPEACHMENT PROBLEMS

Problem 1

On direct examination at trial the Plaintiff has testified to the following:

> I told Brian that my fee would be as little as 3 percent depending on how involved I had to be in putting the deal together. I also told him that I already had a prospect in mind, and if that prospect came through, that I was sure the fee would be on the low end. He said, 'sounds good to me, let's get at it' or something like that. There was no question we had a deal; he was hot to move on the deal.

For the Defendant, conduct the impeachment of Quinlan.

Problem 2

On direct examination at trial the Defendant has testified to the following:

> I told Roberta I really wanted to do this deal myself. When she pressed on, saying she had potential buyers in mind that she wanted to contact, I politely told her to forget it. This was my deal, not hers.

For the Plaintiff, conduct the impeachment of Kane.

Thumbnails of PowerPoint Slides

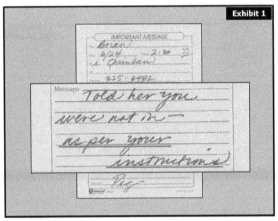

Blank Slide — Slide 1

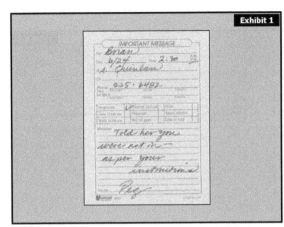

Exhibit 1 — Slide 2

Exhibit 1 — Slide 3

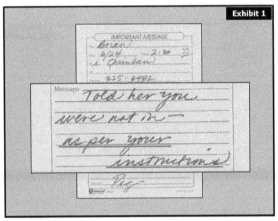

Exhibit 1 — Slide 4

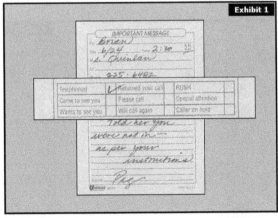

Exhibit 1 — Slide 5

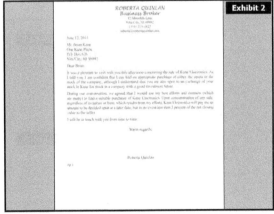

Exhibit 2 — Slide 6

Exhibit 2   Slide 7

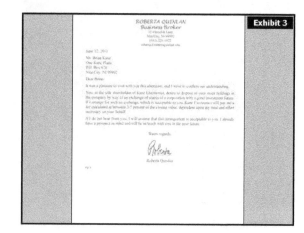

Exhibit 3   Slide 8

Exhibit 3   Slide 9

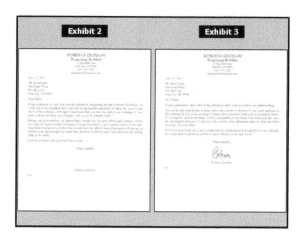

Exhibit 2 & 3   Slide 10

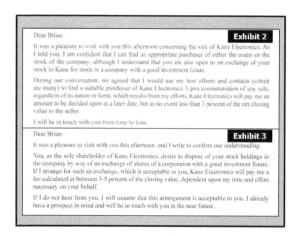

Exhibit 2 & 3   Slide 11

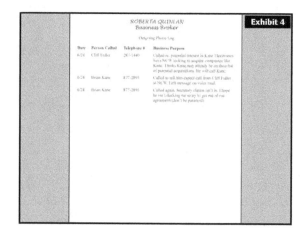

Exhibit 4   Slide 12

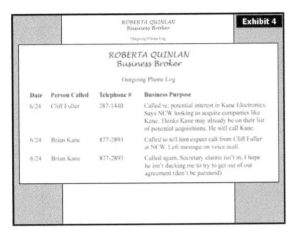

Exhibit 4   Slide 13

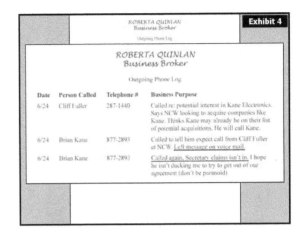

Exhibit 4   Slide 14

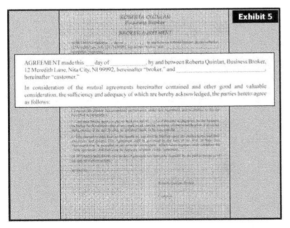

Exhibit 4   Slide 15

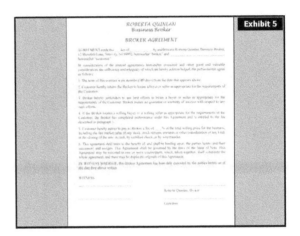

Exhibit 5   Slide 16

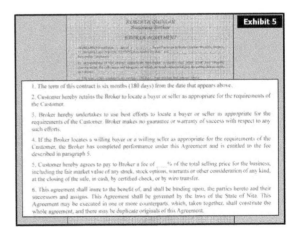

Exhibit 5   Slide 17

Exhibit 5   Slide 18

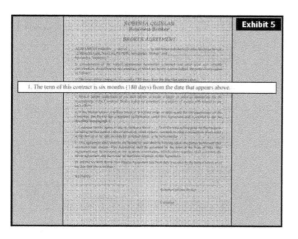

Exhibit 5   Slide 19

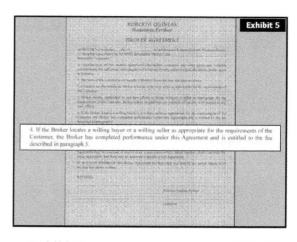

Exhibit 5   Slide 20

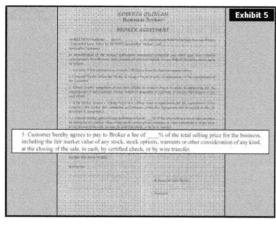

Exhibit 5   Slide 21

Exhibit 5   Slide 22

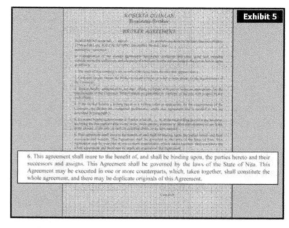

Exhibit 5   Slide 23

Exhibit 5   Slide 24

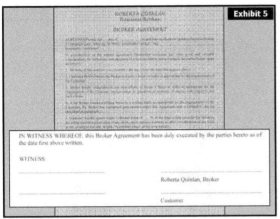

Exhibit 5   Slide 25

Exhibit 6   Slide 26

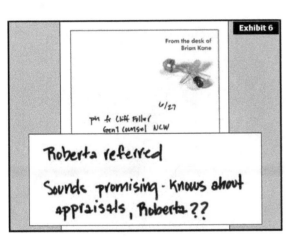

Exhibit 6   Slide 27

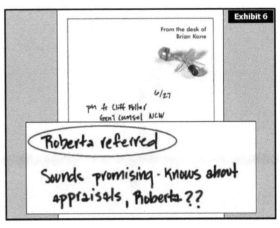

Exhibit 6   Slide 28

Exhibit 7   Slide 29

Exhibit 8   Slide 30

Exhibit 9   Slide 31

Exhibit 10   Slide 32

Exhibit 7 &10   Slide 33

Exhibit 8 & 9   Slide 34

Exhibit 7-10   Slide 35

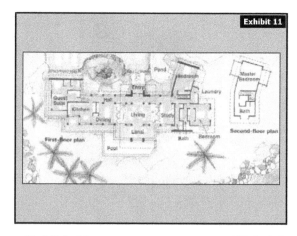

Exhibit 11   Slide 36

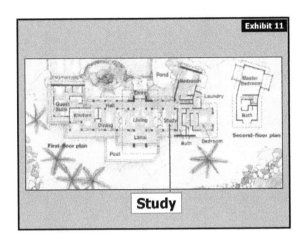

Exhibit 11   Slide 37

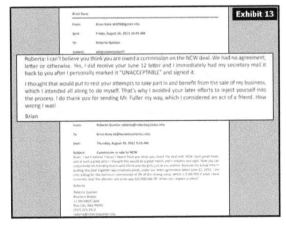

Exhibit 12   Slide 38

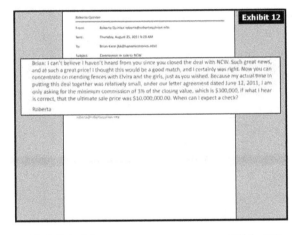

Exhibit 12   Slide 39

Exhibit 13   Slide 40

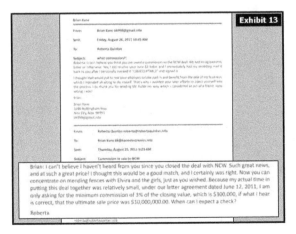

Exhibit 13   Slide 41

Exhibit 13   Slide 42

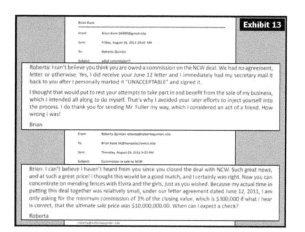

Exhibit 13   Slide 43

Jury Instructions   Slide 44

Jury Instructions   Slide 45

3. As the plaintiff, Roberta Quinlan has the burden of proving her claim by a preponderance of the evidence, which is the greater weight of the evidence or the evidence that you find is more believable.

Jury Instructions   Slide 46

4. To prevail on her claim, the plaintiff, Roberta Quinlan, must show (a) she and Brian Kane made an agreement or contract that she would perform services as a business broker, and he would pay her an agreed amount or the reasonable value of those services, (b) she performed the agreed services, and (c) he failed to pay her the amount due.

Jury Instructions   Slide 47

5. An agreement or contract can be formed by one or more writings, oral statements, or conduct which collectively demonstrates that each of the parties agreed to the same terms.

Jury Instructions   Slide 48

6. When one party offers credible evidence that a letter was correctly addressed and properly mailed in the United States mail, that party is entitled to a rebuttable presumption that the letter was received by the party to whom it was addressed. In this case, the party to whom the letter was addressed has denied receiving it. You, as the trier of fact, must weigh the presumption of receipt against the denial of receipt and decide whether the letter was received.

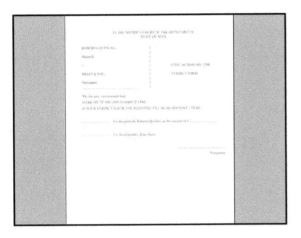

Verdict Form   Slide 49

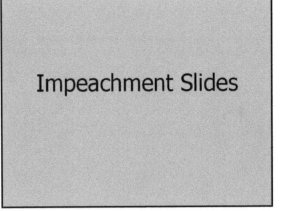

Impeachment Slides   Slide 50

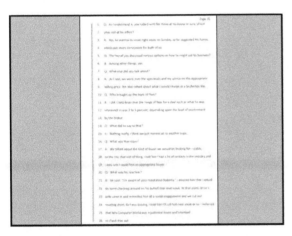

Quinlan Transcript   Slide 51
Page 35, Lines 1-26

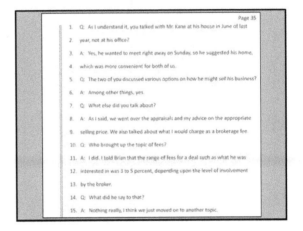

Quinlan Transcript   Slide 52
Page 35, Lines 1-15

Quinlan Video   Slide 53
Page 35, Lines 1-15

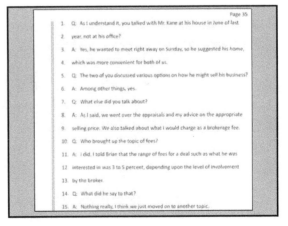

Quinlan Transcript   Slide 54
Page 35, Lines 1-15

Quinlan Video & Transcript   Slide 55
Page 35, Lines 1-15

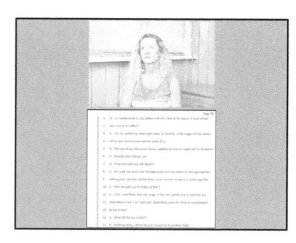

Quinlan Photo & Transcript   Slide 56
Page 35, Lines 1-15

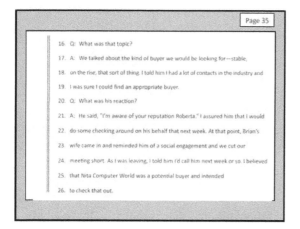

Quinlan Transcript   Slide 57
Page 35, Lines 16-26

Quinlan Video   Slide 58
Page 35, Lines 16-26

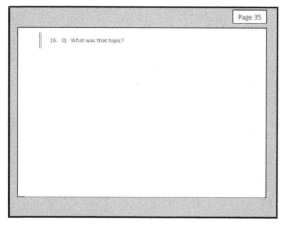

Quinlan Transcript   Slide 59
Page 35, Lines 16-26

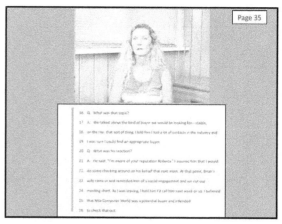

Quinlan Video &Transcript   Slide 60
Page 35, Lines 16-26

Quinlan Video &Transcript   Slide 61
Page 35, Lines 16-26

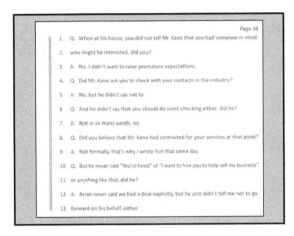

Quinlan Transcript   Slide 62
Page 36, Lines 1-13

Quinlan Video   Slide 63
Page 36, Lines 1-13

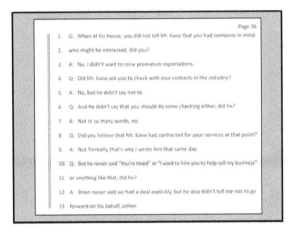

Quinlan Transcript   Slide 64
Page 36, Lines 1-13

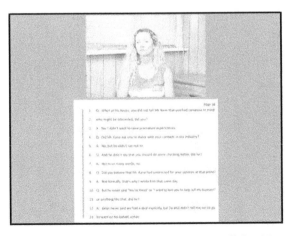

Quinlan Video & Transcript   Slide 65
Page 36, Lines 1-13

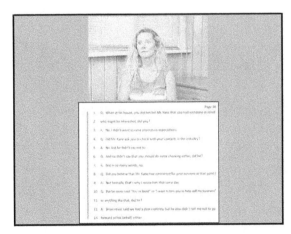

Quinlan Photo & Transcript   Slide 66
Page 36, Lines 1-13

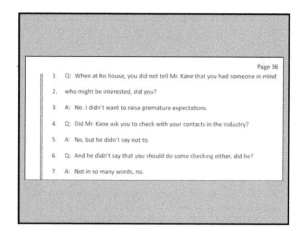

Quinlan Transcript   Slide 67
Page 36, Lines 1-7

Quinlan Video   Slide 68
Page 36, Lines 1-7

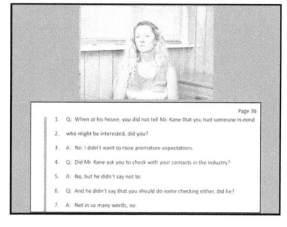

Quinlan Video & Transcript   Slide 69
Page 36, Lines 1-7

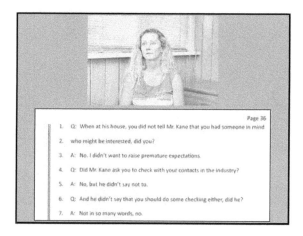

Quinlan Photo & Transcript   Slide 70
Page 36, Lines 1-7

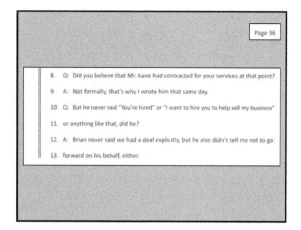

Quinlan Transcript   Slide 71
Page 36, Lines 8-13

Quinlan Video   Slide 72
Page 36, Lines 8-13

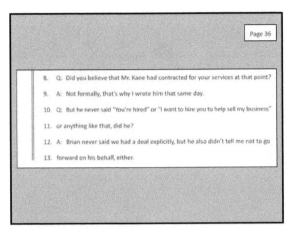

Quinlan Transcript   Slide 73
Page 36, Lines 8-13

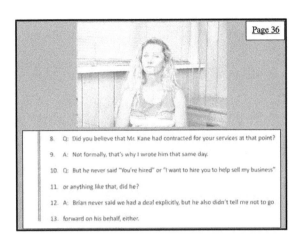

Quinlan Video & Transcript   Slide 74
Page 36, Lines 8-13

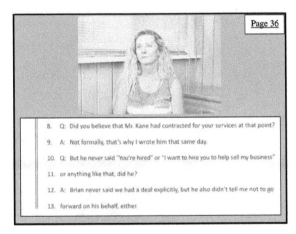

Quinlan Photo & Transcript   Slide 75
Page 36, Lines 8-13

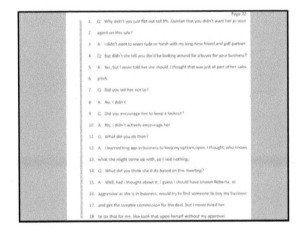

Kane Transcript   Slide 76
Page 22, Lines 1-18

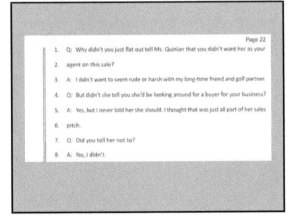

Kane Transcript   Slide 77
Page 22, Lines 1-8

Kane Video   Slide 78
Page 22, Lines 1-8

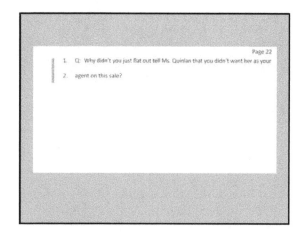

Kane Transcript   Slide 79
Page 22, Lines 1-8

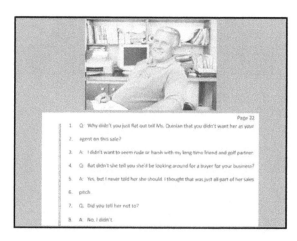

Kane Video & Transcript   Slide 80
Page 22, Lines 1-8

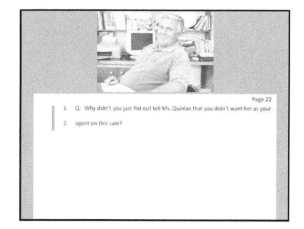

Kane Photo & Transcript   Slide 81
Page 22, Lines 1-8

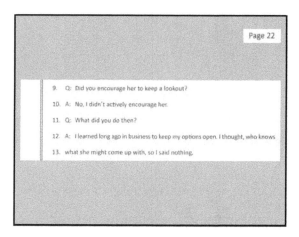

Kane Transcript   Slide 82
Page 22, Lines 9-13

Kane Video   Slide 83
Page 22, Lines 9-13

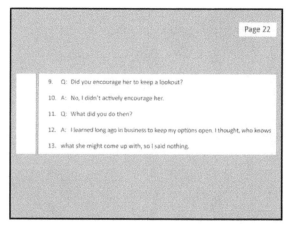

Kane Transcript   Slide 84
Page 22, Lines 9-13

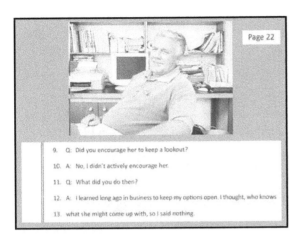

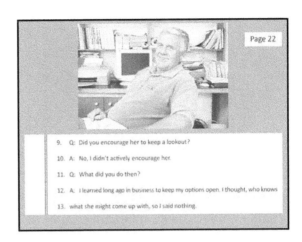

Kane Video & Transcript   Slide 85
Page 22, Lines 9-13

Kane Photo & Transcript   Slide 86
Page 22, Lines 9-13

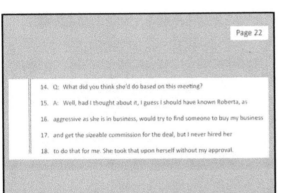

Kane Transcript   Slide 87
Page 22, Lines 14-18

Kane Video   Slide 88
Page 22, Lines 14-18

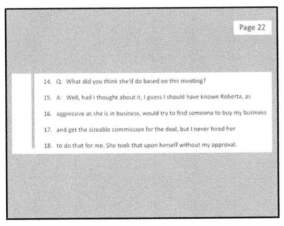

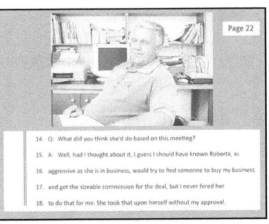

Kane Transcript   Slide 89
Page 22, Lines 14-18

Kane Video & Transcript   Slide 90
Page 22, Lines 14-18

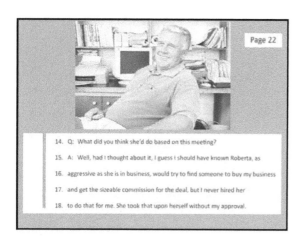

Kane Photo & Transcript   Slide 91
Page 22, Lines 14-18

Persuasion Slides
[with animations]

Persuasion Slides   Slide 92

The Meeting

- Kane's study
- Two hours
- Topic: selling business
- Reviewed alternatives
- Kane's goal: sell
- Quinlan's business: selling

The Meeting   Slide 93

The Contract

- ☑ Quinlan required to find a buyer
- ☑ Kane had choice to accept the buyer
- ☑ If Quinlan's buyer accepted, fee due
- ☑ Fee set at 3-5% depending on effort
- ☑ Payment due at closing

The Contract   Slide 94

Three Key Questions

1. Was there an agreement?

2. Did Roberta Quinlan perform the agreed services?

3. Did Brian Kane pay what he owed?

Three questions   Slide 95

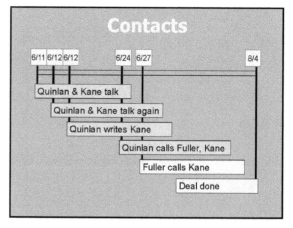

Timeline-Contacts   Slide 96

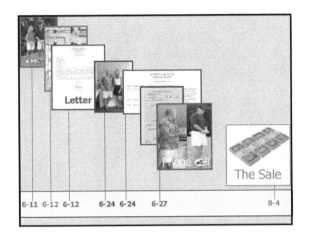

Timeline II   Slide 97

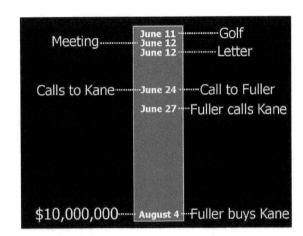

Timeline III   Slide 98

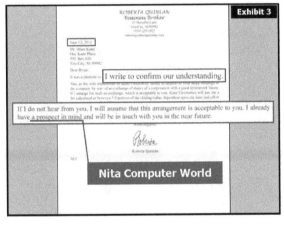

Exhibit 3   Slide 99

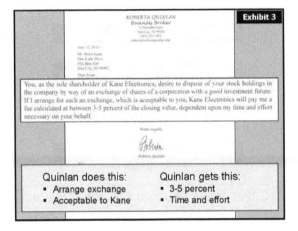

Exhibit 3   Slide 100

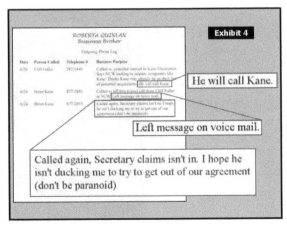

Exhibit 4   Slide 101

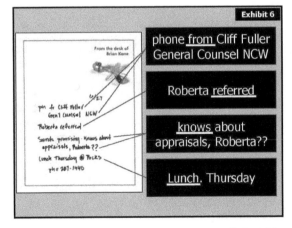

Exhibit 6   Slide 102

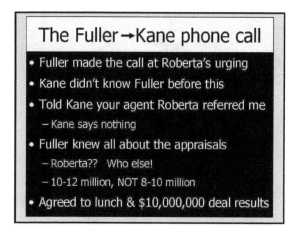

Fuller to Kane call   Slide 103

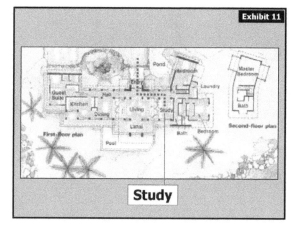

Exhibit 11   Slide 104

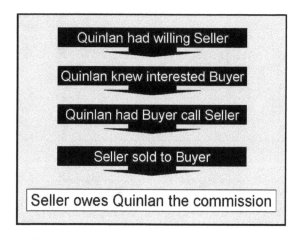

Relationship chart   Slide 105

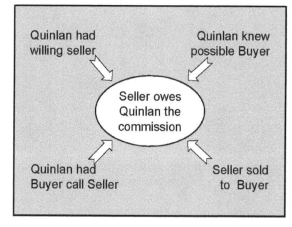

All roads lead to Rome   Slide 106

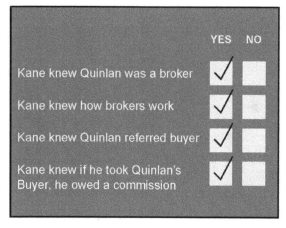

Checklist   Slide 107

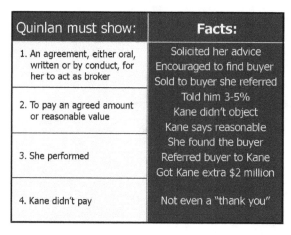

Quinlan must show   Slide 108

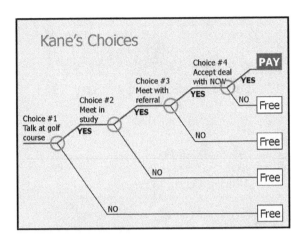

Kane's choices   Slide 109

The Quinlan connection   Slide 110

The Quinlan connection II   Slide 111

The Quinlan connection III   Slide 112

The Quinlan connection IV   Slide 113

Kane quote   Slide 114

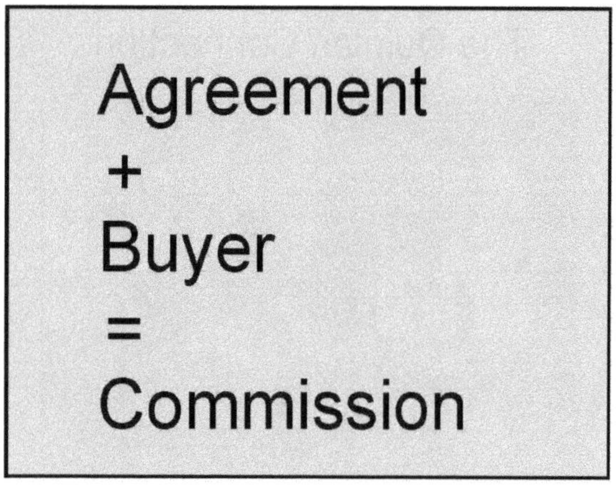
Agreement
+
Buyer
=
Commission

A + B = C Slide 115

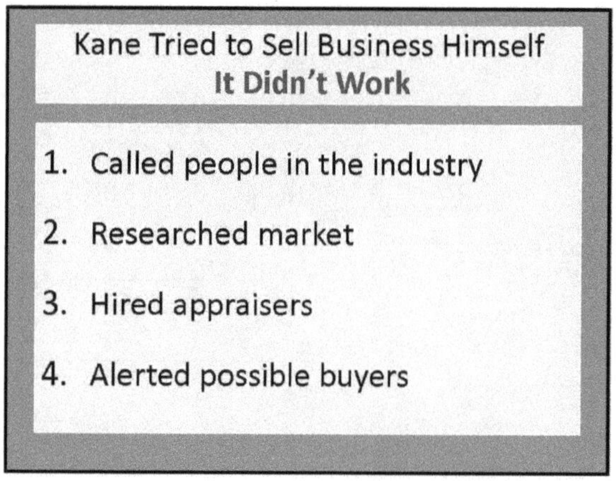
Kane Tried to Sell Business Himself
It Didn't Work
1. Called people in the industry
2. Researched market
3. Hired appraisers
4. Alerted possible buyers

It didn't work Slide 116

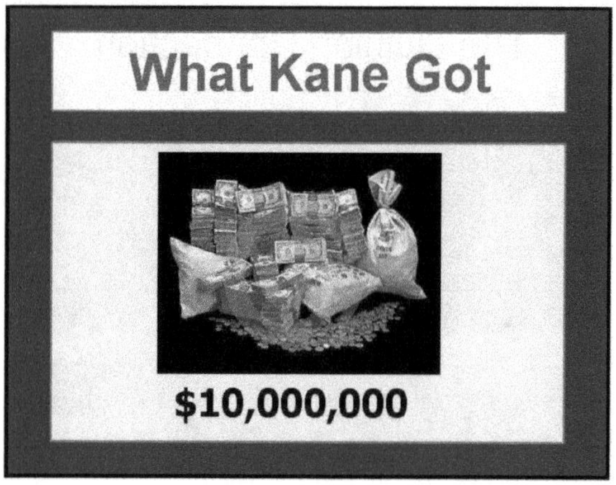
What Kane Got
$10,000,000

What Kane got Slide 117

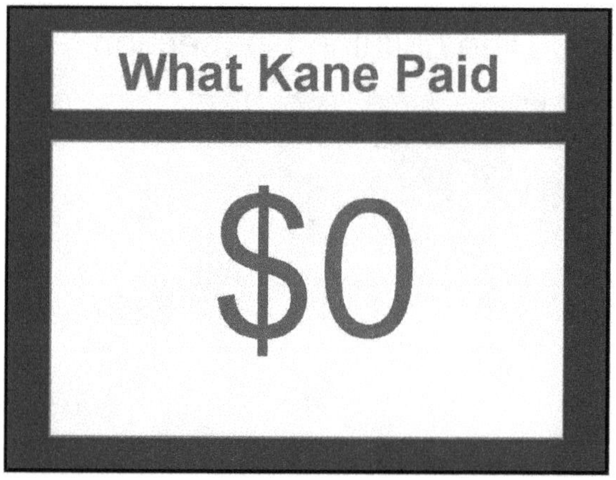
What Kane Paid
$0

What Kane paid Slide 118

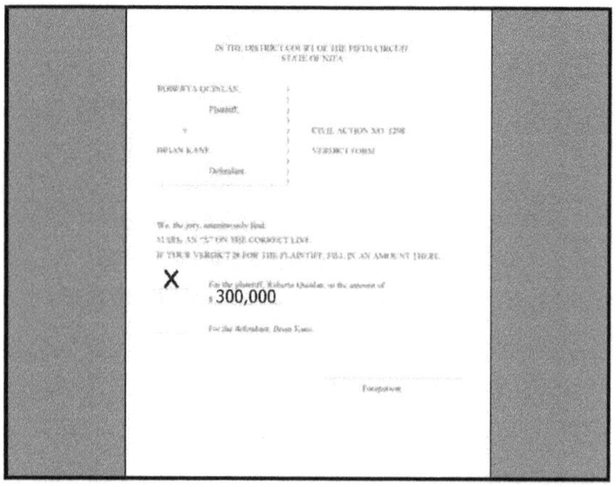
X
300,000

Verdict form Slide 119

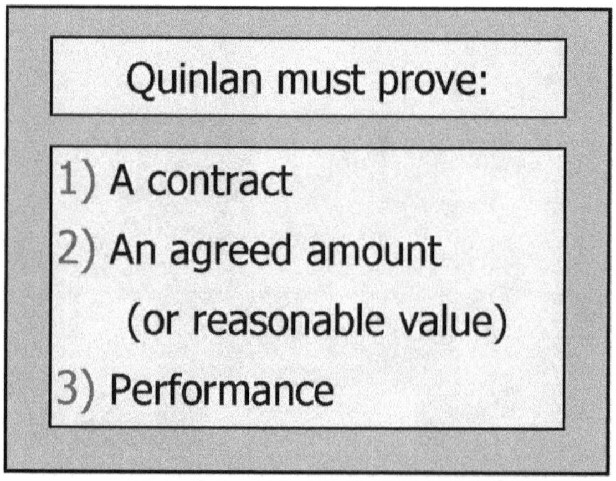
Quinlan must prove:
1) A contract
2) An agreed amount
(or reasonable value)
3) Performance

Quinlan must prove Slide 120

A Contract?

- No broker agreement
- No "you've got a deal"
- No signature by Kane

A Contract?   Slide 121

An agreed amount?

- Between 3-5 percent
  - Closing value
- To be decided later
- At least 3%
  - Net closing value

An Agreement?   Slide 122

A Contract is
THIS IS NOT TWO PEOPLE AGREEING:
two people agreeing on the same terms

Mr. Kane
- Never said check with your contacts
- Never said had a deal
- Never said I want to hire you
- Never said you're hired

Ms. Quinlan
- Never said she had a buyer in mind
- When Quinlan left she did not believe Kane had formally contracted for her services

Two people agreeing   Slide 123

A Contract?

4. Q: Did Mr. Kane ask you to check with your contacts in the industry?
5. A: No, but he didn't say not to.

A Contract?   Slide 124

A Contract?

6. Q: And he didn't say that you should do some checking either, did he?
7. A: Not in so many words, no.

A Contract? II   Slide 125

A Contract?

8. Q: Did you believe that Mr. Kane had contracted for your services at that point?
9. A: Not formally, that's why I wrote him that same day.

A Contract? III   Slide 126

Slide 127 — A Contract? IV

A Contract?

10. Q: But he never said "You're hired" or "I want to hire you to help sell my business"
11. or anything like that, did he?
12. A: Brian never said we had a deal explicitly, but he also didn't tell me not to go
13. forward on his behalf, either.

A Contract? IV   Slide 127

Slide 128 — A Contract? V

A Contract?

8. Q: Did you believe that Mr. Kane had contracted for your services at that point?
9. A: Not formally, that's why I wrote him that same day.
10. Q: But he never said "You're hired" or "I want to hire you to help sell my business"
11. or anything like that, did he?
12. A: Brian never said we had a deal explicitly, but he also didn't tell me not to go
13. forward on his behalf, either.

A Contract? V   Slide 128

Slide 129 — Quinlan must prove II

Quinlan must (prove):

	Yes	No
1. Had contract		■
2. Performed		■
3. Not paid		■

Quinlan must prove II   Slide 129

Slide 130 — Plaintiff's "Facts"

Plaintiff's "Facts"

1. Kane agreed to a broker *(NOT TRUE)*
2. Quinlan didn't get Kane's letter *(NOT TRUE)*
3. Broker worked on the deal *(NOT TRUE)*
4. $300,000 a fair commission *(NOT TRUE)*

Plaintiff's "Facts"   Slide 130

Slide 131 — Where is the evidence?

Where is the evidence?

1. Kane agreed to a broker
2. Quinlan didn't get Kane's letter
3. Broker did work on the deal
4. $300,000 is a fair commission

Where is the evidence?   Slide 131

Slide 132 — Acting as a broker?

WAS QUINLAN ACTING AS A BROKER DOES?

Events	Was Quinlan There?
- Introduction	NO
- Lunch	NO
- President	NO
- Lawyers	NO
- When price determined	NO
- Any of the 10 meetings	NO
- Closing	NO

Acting as a broker?   Slide 132

Relationship chart   Slide 133

Contract = 2 people agree   Slide 134

No Contract   Slide 135

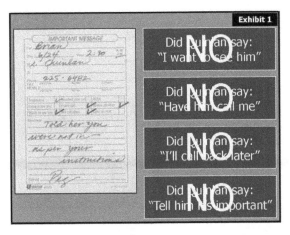

Flying check marks   Slide 136

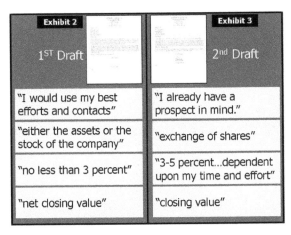

Side-by-side comparison   Slide 137

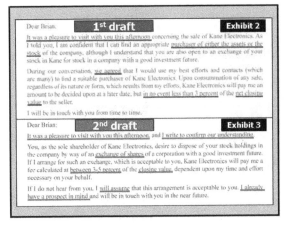

Bottom-top comparison   Slide 138

Quinlan quote   Slide 139

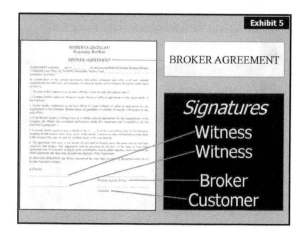

Exhibit 5 signatures   Slide 140

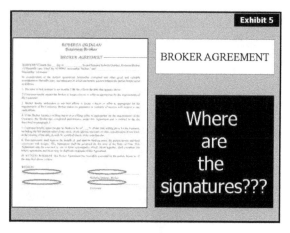

Where are the signatures?   Slide 141

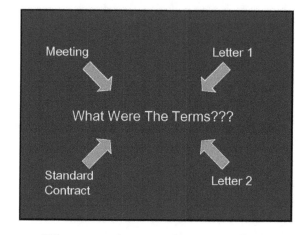

What were the terms?   Slide 142

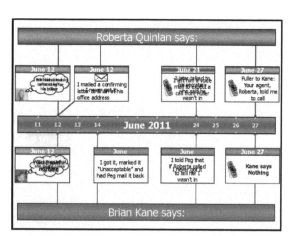

She says, he says   Slide 143

CPSIA information can be obtained
at www.ICGtesting.com
Printed in the USA
FSHW021600100119
54912FS